D1388900

Seriously Sexy & Senior

Seriously Sexy & Senior

HOW TO SHOW YOU'VE STILL GOT SPARKLE

This edition published in 2016
by Baker & Taylor UK Ltd
Bicester, Oxfordshire OX26 4ST

Written by Roffy
Cover illustration by Kirsten Ulve
Contents illustrations by Lindsey Sagar
Contents layout: seagulls.net
Design: Milestone Creative

ISBN: 978-1-910562-78-9

Printed in China by Everbest Printing Investment Ltd

Welcome
sexy seniors!

There is a time in life when you face a crossroads and need to make a choice. Do you choose to mature like a fine wine, or start growing old disgracefully?

Let's face it, those around you expect the former, but you want to do the latter.

Whichever road you choose to take (the latter...) we know you will stay young at heart and sexy with it. While there isn't a complete roadmap to guide your every step, we have sought out some words of wisdom from women of all ages and walks of life to help you set off on the right foot.

And remember – as Katharine Hepburn so wisely observed – if you obey all the rules, you miss all the fun.

NUMBER 23

After a round of golf, a husband returned to his sexy senior wife with some juicy gossip. "I heard that the security guard has slept with all the women on our retirement complex except one."

The wife said, "That must be Nancy at number 23 – no one likes her."

WHY IT'S GREAT TO BE A

Senior Lady...

The clothes you've put away until they come back in style have come back in style.

Your secrets are safe with your friends because they can't remember them.

There's nothing left to learn the hard way.

Your aching joints know it's going to rain before the Met Office does.

Dating someone half your age isn't breaking any laws.

You don't need so much to drink any more – you get the same effect standing up.

Even I don't wake up looking like Cindy Crawford.

CINDY CRAWFORD

FOR A YOUNG MAN TO START HIS CAREER WITH A LOVE AFFAIR WITH AN OLDER WOMAN WAS QUITE DE RIGUEUR... OF COURSE, IT MUST NOT GO ON FOR TOO LONG. AN APPRENTICESHIP WAS A VERY DIFFERENT THING FROM A CAREER.

VITA SACKVILLE-WEST

OUT OF THE MOUTHS OF BABES

Sometimes it's the little ones that say the funniest things. Let's take a look at a few genuine inter-generational exchanges.

I was in the bathroom, putting on my make-up, under the watchful eyes of my young granddaughter, as I'd done many times before. After I'd applied my lipstick and started to leave, the little one said, "But Grandma, you forgot to kiss the toilet paper goodbye!"

My young grandson called the other day to wish me happy birthday. He asked me how old I was, and I told him, 72. My grandson was quiet for a moment, and then he asked, "Did you start at 1?"

I was testing my granddaughter on her colours. I pointed to several things in the room and she got the colour right every time. I was enjoying it, but eventually I pointed at one too many things and she said, "Grandma, I think you should try to figure out some of these colours yourself!"

When my grandson asked me how old I was, I teasingly replied, "I'm not sure."
"Look in your underwear, Grandma," he advised. "Mine says I'm 4 to 6."

My 7-year-old grandson told me about a recent school lesson. "Grandma, we learned how to make babies."

I was a little surprised, but decided to find out more. "That's interesting. How do you make babies?"

"It's simple," he replied. "You just change 'y' to 'i' and add 'es'."

I was telling my little granddaughter about my own childhood. "We used to skate on the village pond. I made all the furniture in my doll's house. I rode ponies on the beach. We picked wild berries in the woods."

The little girl was wide-eyed, taking this all in. At last she said, "I sure wish I'd met you a lot sooner!"

I was looking after my granddaughter, Lucy, for an afternoon. She was so sweet, but I had a devil of a time getting her to drink her water. After some encouragement, she finally drank it down and I told her how happy I was.

When her mother came to pick her up, Lucy announced, "Drinking makes Granny happy!"

I was cleaning my dentures in the bathroom while my grandson watched me intently. He sat riveted as I took them out, brushed and rinsed them, and then popped them back in.

"Cool, Grandma!" he said.
"Now take off your arm and clean it."

GUY JUST CAME UP TO ME AND SAID, "WHAT'S YOUR FAVOURITE POSITION?" I REPLIED, "CEO."

MICHELLE MONE

BROKEN OFF

Ruby and Sally were having lunch together. Ruby said, "I hear you broke off your engagement to Harold. Why?"

"My feelings towards him aren't the same any more."

"Are you returning the ring?"

"No! My feelings towards the ring haven't changed."

The secret of staying young is to live honestly, eat slowly, and lie about your age.

LUCILLE BALL

• SEXY TIP •

Don't spend too much time on the sunbed, otherwise it will literally be your golden age.

The proverbials

Proverbs provide timeless advice. Here are a few of our favourites for the sexy senior to live by:

It's better to arrive late than arrive ugly.

....

One good turn gets most of the blankets.

....

Love your neighbour, but don't get caught.

....

Old age is always 15 years older than you are.

....

A hard man is good to find.

Experience is a wonderful thing. It enables you to recognize a mistake when you make it again.

....

If the shoe fits, buy them in every colour.

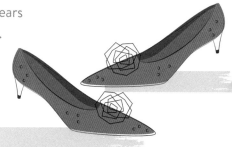

> *HOW MANY HUSBANDS HAVE I HAD? YOU MEAN APART FROM MY OWN?*
>
> **ZSA ZSA GABOR**

Living in sin

Sarah and June met at an engagement party for a mutual friend's daughter. They got chatting about the couple and the fact that they had been living with each other for five years before deciding to get married.

"I don't know," said June, "that sort of thing didn't happen in my day. I didn't sleep with my husband before we were married. Did you?"

"I don't know," said Sarah, "what's his name?"

It's just a number

As Joan Collins once said, "Age is just a number. It's totally irrelevant unless, of course, you happen to be a bottle of wine..."

A sexy senior lady like you knows that you're not as young as you used to be, but it's nowhere near time to give up on life yet.

YOU MIGHT BE...

TOO OLD FOR:	BUT TOO YOUNG FOR:
Breakdancing	Tea dancing
Bieber	Bygraves
Wet T-shirt Contest	Wet Shawl Contest
Raving till 4am	Dinner at 4pm
Sowing wild oats	Filing hard corns

14

WOULD YOU BELIEVE...

By the time you reach seventy, you are likely to have swallowed between two and three kilograms of lipstick.

Mind Your Own Business

A senior, sexy and smartly dressed woman is sitting at a bar. A man approaches her.

"Good evening, my darling," he says. "Would you like a little company?"

"Why?" asks the woman. "Do you have one to sell?"

Essential reading

Whether you are already living with your man or about to move in with a new beau, they occasionally need reminding that they share the house. Just because he's been around the block a few times, he's still a man.

Here are some suggested books to place on the coffee table to keep him in line.

The Infinite Toilet Roll: Fact or Myth?

....

I Can Go Shopping Without Moaning – You Can Too!

....

No-one Got Shot for Tidying Up

....

Unloading the Dishwasher – Less Complicated than Tidying the Shed

....

Bang on Target: Near the Laundry Basket is not the same as In the Laundry Basket

....

FUNNY REALLY. WHEN YOU LOOK AT THE THINGS THAT GO ON THESE DAYS, MY STORY READS LIKE NODDY.

DIANA DORS

IN THE NEWS – GO BO!

Is Bo Gilbert, from Alcester, Warwickshire, the Sexiest Senior in the UK? She modelled for June 2016 edition Vogue magazine at the age of 100!

She was chosen by Harvey Nichols for a special campaign to celebrate the magazine's 100th anniversary.

· SEXY TIP ·

Remember to let your hair down sometimes. Just don't forget to pick it up again.

THAT'S THE AWFUL THING ABOUT DATING. TIGHT UNDERWEAR. WE WOULD ALL LIKE TO BE IN A BIG BRA AND PANTS AND WHEN YOU ARE IN A SECURE RELATIONSHIP YOU CAN DO THAT.

DAWN FRENCH

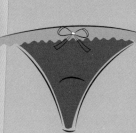

Senior Gentleman: "Where have you been all my life?"

Sexy Senior Lady: "For the first half of it, I wasn't even born."

Relax, gentlemen…

A SEXY SENIOR LADY WILL NEVER
ACCUSE YOU OF STEALING THE
BEST YEARS OF HER LIFE – BECAUSE
CHANCES ARE HER EX-HUSBAND
ALREADY DID THAT.

IF A MAN IS BALD IN FRONT,
HE'S A THINKER. IF HE'S BALD AT
THE BACK, HE'S A LOVER. IF HE'S
BALD BOTH FRONT AND BACK,
HE THINKS HE'S A LOVER.

Wishing on a starter

Jean and Arthur were celebrating their 50th wedding anniversary at their favourite restaurant when a tiny fairy appeared on their table.

She said, "For being such a wonderful, devoted couple for all this time, I will grant you each a wish."

"Oh how lovely," said Jean. "I would love to travel around the world with my darling husband."

The fairy waved her magic wand and – *poof* – two tickets for the Queen Mary II appeared in her hands.

Arthur thought for a moment, then said, "OK, an opportunity like this will never come again. I'm sorry Jean, but I wish for a wife 30 years younger than me."

Jean and the fairy were both deeply disappointed, but the fairy was compelled to honour the wish. She waved her magic wand and – *poof* – Arthur became 122 years old.

The moral of this story... be careful what you wish for.

Never say never, but there are not enough hours in the day!

MICHELLE MONE

A successful man is one who makes more money than his wife can spend. A successful woman is one who can find such a man.

LANA TURNER

When you're 16,
30 seems ancient.
When you're 30,
45 seems ancient.
When you're 45,
60 seems ancient.
When you're 60,
nothing seems ancient.

HELEN MIRREN

22

> **· SEXY TIP ·**
>
> Laugh a lot – that way your wrinkles
> will be in the right places.

Vexed text

A couple in their later years would often text each
other on their phones. One day, the wife decided
to send her husband something romantic:

If you are sleeping, send me your dreams.
If you are laughing, send me your smile.
If you are eating, send me a bite.
If you are drinking, send me a sip.
If you are crying, send me your tears.

The husband wrote back:
I'm on the toilet. Please advise.

IN THE NEWS – POLLING STATION

A recent survey asked a group of seniors what their partner did that turned them off during sex. Some interesting answers came back, including:

Watching television
Forgetting their name
Online shopping

A WOMAN IS LIKE A TEA BAG.
YOU NEVER KNOW HOW STRONG
IT IS UNTIL IT'S IN HOT WATER.

ELEANOR ROOSEVELT

Classic proposal

87-year-old Lloyd had fallen deeply in love with June, a mere 11 years his junior. One afternoon, after watching a classic romantic film on the television, he got down on one knee in front of her.

"June," said Lloyd.

"Oh, Lloyd," said June with a twinkle in her eye.

"June, I have two questions to ask you," continued Lloyd. "Will you marry me?"

"Oh, yes Lloyd, yes!" replied June excitedly. "But what's your second question?"

"Will you help me get up?"

WINE DOESN'T MAKE US ANY YOUNGER. NEITHER DOES CARROT JUICE. WINE IT IS THEN.

> **· SEXY TIP ·**
>
> There are plenty of fish in the sea
> – just find a good hook

I HAVEN'T TRUSTED POLLS SINCE I READ THAT 62% OF WOMEN HAD AFFAIRS DURING THEIR LUNCH HOUR. I'VE NEVER MET A WOMAN IN MY LIFE WHO WOULD GIVE UP LUNCH FOR SEX.

ERMA BOMBECK

At a cocktail party, one woman
said to another, "Aren't you wearing
your wedding ring on the wrong finger?"

The other replied, "Yes I am.
I married the wrong man."

What's Good for the Goose ...

A Sexy Senior recently married a widower.
A friend remarked, "I suppose your husband
sometimes talks about his first wife?"

"Oh, not any more, he doesn't," she replied.

"What stopped him?"

"I started talking about my next husband."

*I DON'T EXERCISE
BECAUSE IT MAKES THE
ICE JUMP RIGHT OUT
OF MY GLASS.*

A police officer saw a Sexy Senior
driving and knitting at the same time.
After driving next to her for a while
he yells to her, "PULLOVER".
She replies, "No, pair of socks!"

27

New romantics

An older couple were lying in bed one night.
The husband was falling asleep but the wife was in a
romantic mood and wanted to talk.

She said, "You used to hold my hand
when we were courting."

Wearily he reached across, held her hand for
a second and then tried to get back to sleep.

A few moments later she said,
"Then you used to kiss me."

Mildly irritated, he reached across, gave her a peck on
the cheek and settled down again to sleep.

Thirty seconds later she said,
"Then you used to bite my neck."

Angrily, he threw back the bed clothes
and got out of bed.

"Where are you going?" she asked.

"To get my teeth!"

At every party there are two kinds of people – those who want to go home and those who don't. The trouble is, they are usually married to each other.

ANN LANDERS

My mother told me you don't have to put anything in your mouth you don't want to. Then she made me eat broccoli, which felt like double standards.

SARAH MILLICAN

Old wine and friends improve with age.

ITALIAN PROVERB

· SEXY TIP ·

If you have to choose between two evils,
always pick the one you haven't tried before.

AT MY AGE, I'VE SEEN IT ALL.
THANKFULLY, I'VE FORGOTTEN
MOST OF IT SO I'M READY TO
SEE IT ALL AGAIN.

Away day

Alice and Steve had found love in later life and had recently moved in together. They were on a train taking them on a romantic weekend for the first time since moving in when Alice exclaimed, "Oh god, Steve, I left the oven on!"

"Don't worry Alice," he replied, "the house won't burn down. I left the bath running."

THE BODY IS LIKE A CAR: THE OLDER YOU BECOME THE MORE CARE YOU HAVE TO TAKE OF IT – AND YOU DON'T LEAVE A FERRARI OUT IN THE SUN.

JOAN COLLINS

Why do men like smart women? Opposites attract.

Smack down

A sexy senior was telling her daughter about a date with a man who was somewhat more senior himself.

"Believe it or not, I had to slap his face three times!" said the woman.

"Blimey, was he trying to get fresh with you?" the daughter asked in disgust.

"Oh, no," her mother explained. "We were in bed already. I had to keep slapping his face to keep him awake!"

NOW I'VE LEARNED THE RULES OF LIFE, I THINK I'LL INVENT MY OWN GAME.

Perky pills

Young Simon had been a little out of sorts recently, feeling tired and lethargic. His grandfather, Graham, came to see him and was glad to see that Simon was looking much better.

"You're looking fighting fit now, what sorted you out?" asked Graham.

"I rested up for a couple of days, but I think it was these pills that made the difference. I feel so invigorated every time I take one," said Simon.

"Interesting," said his grandfather. "I don't suppose I could have a few of those could I? I'm a little short right now, but I could give you a fiver for them next time I see you."

Simon said that was fine and gave him a few pills.

They met up again a week later, and grandfather Graham clearly had a whole new spring in his step. "Simon, good to see you!" he said. "Here's a tenner for those marvellous pills you gave me."

"Cheers Grandad, but I'm sure we agreed a fiver for them," said Simon.

"Yes, but there's another five from your grandmother."

A Sexy Senior told her portrait artist "Paint me with diamond earrings, a diamond necklace, emerald bracelets, a ruby broach, and gold Rolex."

"But you aren't wearing any of those things" replied the artist.

"I know, but if my husband should remarry I want his new wife to go crazy looking for the jewelry."

I refuse to think of them as chin hairs. I think of them as stray eyebrows.

JANETTE BARBER

There is an element of seduction in shoes that doesn't exist for men. A woman can be sexy, charming, witty or shy with her shoes.

CHRISTIAN LOUBOUTIN

New man

Two sexy seniors, Jenny and Susan, were meeting up for lunch. Jenny asked Susan, "So Susan, how is it going with your new fellow?"

"Jim?" said Susan. "He's charming. We've been seeing each other for a few months now and he always calls me such endearing things – honey, my love, darling, sweetheart, you know."

"Ah," said Jenny, "that's sweet."

"I thought so too," said Susan, "but he's getting on a bit, and now I think he's just forgotten my name."

An archaeologist is the best husband any woman can have: the older she gets, the more interested he is in her.

AGATHA CHRISTIE

· SEXY TIP ·

Be positive – don't let today be a
total waste of make-up.

A SENIOR AND A GENTLEMAN

A senior gentleman, very well dressed, hair well groomed, great-looking suit, flower in his lapel and with a hint of fine aftershave, walked into an upscale cocktail lounge.

Sitting at the bar was one sexy senior lady.

The gentleman walked over, sat alongside her, ordered a drink for himself and one for her, took a sip, turned to her and said, "So tell me, do I come here often?"

I DON'T KNOW WHY PEOPLE ARE SO OBSESSED WITH AGE ANYWAY. I MEAN, 90 IS THE NEW 70; 70 IS THE NEW 50 AND 50 IS THE NEW 40; SO THE WHOLE ACT-YOUR-AGE THING? ONLY UP TO A POINT.

JOAN COLLINS

Eventually you will
reach a point when
you stop lying about
your age and start
bragging about it.

I FEEL LESS PRESSURE TO DRESS YOUTHFULLY. I'M 50 AND EVERYONE KNOWS I'M 50 – WHO ARE YOU KIDDING? JEANS ARE MY UNIFORM. I HAVE ABOUT 15 PAIRS.

MICHELLE PFEIFFER

TOP 10 FABULOUS OVER-50S

No, we can't believe these seriously hot ladies are over 50 either!

Michelle Pfeiffer
Elizabeth Hurley
Cindy Crawford
Sharon Stone
Kim Cattrall
Elle Macpherson
Julianne Moore
Christie Brinkley
Madonna
Demi Moore

TOP 10 SEXY OVER-60S

These sexy dames just keep getting better with age!

Dame Helen Mirren
Susan Sarandon
Joan Collins
Raquel Welch
Goldie Hawn
Joanna Lumley
Jessica Lange
Diana Ross
Sigourney Weaver
Catherine Deneuve

I am not too keen on my nose, I don't like my knees, I hate my ankles, I am unsure about my behind, I don't like my legs at all. I am not too sure about my chin, my forehead is a bit dodgy. But, overall, I can live with it.

DAME HELEN MIRREN

What to wear

Two sexy senior ladies were discussing the upcoming dance at the country club.

"The invitation says that we're supposed to wear something that matches our husband's hair, so that means I'm wearing black," said Mrs Jackson.

"Oh good lord," said Mrs Johnson, "I'd better not go."

FASHION MAY NOT BE A WEAPON OF THE WOMAN BUT AT LEAST IT GIVES HER THE AMMUNITION.

BRIGITTE BARDOT

· *SEXY TIP* ·

If anyone says you look like mutton dressed
as lamb, tell them Heston Blumenthal
is your stylist.

Sexy reads

Put down your Aga Saga or back away from
Fifty Shades of Grey. Take a step back in time to the
70s and 80s, when the phrase "bonkbuster" was
invented. Which of these outrageous best-sellers
do you remember from back in the day?

Lace, Shirley Conran

Riders, Jilly Cooper

Hollywood Wives, Jackie Collins

Scruples, Shirley Conran

If Tomorrow Comes, Sidney Sheldon

IF HIGH HEELS WERE SO WONDERFUL, MEN WOULD BE WEARING THEM.

SUE GRAFTON

Retirement means goodbye tension, hello pension!

Give it up!

Ladies, you are happy and confident in your years,
but is he? Here are the sure-fire signs that
he is trying a bit too hard:

There is more hair dye on his collar than on his hair.

Wearing jeans, but still with the waistband above his belly button.

His spray tan finishes half an inch lower than his hairline.

Mentioning Kim Kardashian in a sentence that doesn't begin, "Sorry but who is...?"

Using the word "hip" to describe anything other than a recent operation.

Driving an open-top sports car, even though it's never gone above 35 mph.

Owning the latest smartphone but with no idea how to use it.

Referring to websites as "the Youtube", "the Facebook" and "the eBay".

Talking about any programme on Channel 5.

Ponytail!

LUCKY FOR SOME...
SEVEN FAMOUS COUGAR COUPLES

These relationships may not have stood the test of time, but these experienced Hollywood ladies probably taught their younger boyfriends a thing or two!

Susan Sarandon and Tim Robbins
Age difference – 12 years

Courtney Cox and Johnny McDaid
Age difference – 12 years

Demi Moore and Ashton Kutcher
Age difference – 15 years

Sandra Bullock and Ryan Gosling
Age difference – 16 years

Jennifer Lopez and Caspar Smart
Age difference – 18 years

Elizabeth Taylor and Larry Fortensky
Age difference – 20 years

Joan Collins and Percy Gibson
Age difference – 32 years

I'm old enough to know better. That makes it even more fun!

I'D MARRY AGAIN IF I FOUND A MAN WHO HAD FIFTEEN MILLION DOLLARS, WOULD SIGN OVER HALF TO ME, AND GUARANTEE THAT HE'D BE DEAD WITHIN A YEAR.

BETTE DAVIS

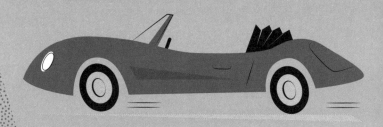

TOP 10 BEST OF BRITISH MEN

Eye candy with a British accent for
the discerning older lady!

Daniel Craig

Sean Connery

Liam Neeson

Hugh Grant

Benedict Cumberbatch

Tom Hiddleston

Sean Bean

Charles Dance

Paul Hollywood

Daniel Day-Lewis

The moment you try to be sexy, then it's not.

DANIEL CRAIG

PENGUINS MATE FOR LIFE. WHICH DOESN'T REALLY SURPRISE ME, BECAUSE THEY ALL LOOK EXACTLY ALIKE. IT'S NOT LIKE THEY'RE GONNA MEET A BETTER-LOOKING PENGUIN SOMEDAY.

ELLEN DEGENERES

VINTAGE WHINE

A couple in their 60s are enjoying a bottle of Merlot in the garden when she says, "I love you."

He asks, "Is that you or the wine talking?"

She replies, "It's me... talking to the wine."

MEN TALK – PART I

Every now and then, men say something worth listening to. Let's hear some of their thoughts on things senior and/or sexy.

If somebody says: "You were voted the world's sexiest man," I have no idea what that means. How do I respond? "Thank you" is the best you can do. George Clooney is the world's sexiest man, anyway.

DANIEL CRAIG

My wife met me at the door the other night in a sexy negligee. Unfortunately, she was just coming home.

RODNEY DANGERFIELD

Nothing risqué, nothing gained.

ALEXANDER WOOLLCOTT

I think trying too hard to be sexy is the worst thing in the world a woman can do.

CHRISTIAN BALE

It's the only thing sexier than a sexy woman. A sexy woman cooking sausages.

RODDY DOYLE

According to a new survey, women say they feel more comfortable undressing in front of men than they do undressing in front of other women. They say that women are too judgmental, where, of course, men are just grateful.

ROBERT DE NIRO

Well-behaved women seldom make history.

LAUREL THATCHER ULRICH

QUESTION TIME

A doctor was meeting a new senior lady patient for the first time and had a few questions. He started with, "How long have you been bedridden?"

After a look of shock, then confusion, she answered, "Why, not for about twenty years – when my husband was alive."

GOLDEN LINES

You remember Blanche from The Golden Girls, one of the cheekier US imports from the 80s? But did you know her full name was Blanche Elizabeth Devereaux, making her initials B. E. D.? Here are a few of our favourite lines from one of TV's sexiest seniors.

I swear with God as my witness, I will never pick up another man!... in a library... on a Saturday... unless he's cute... and drives a nice car... Amen.

I was entertaining a gentleman caller. She walked in on me at the most inopportune time. I could have lost my balance and chipped a tooth.

Like I'm the only person who's ever mixed a margarita in a sailor's mouth.

You know how fragile men's egos are. Do the smallest thing like scream out the wrong name and they go to pieces.

Dorothy: How long do you think you can stay handcuffed?
Blanche: My personal best is 32 hours... of course, then I had someone to play with.

Blanche: My God, you're Mr Burt Reynolds.
Burt Reynolds: I sure hope so. If not, I've got the wrong underwear on.

WWJD? (WHAT WOULD JOAN DO?)

Senior crisis of confidence? Let's find out what super-hot senior, Dame Joan Collins has to say!

I don't have time to exercise. WWJD?

"Doing 20 minutes of stretching, light weights and floor exercises three times a week takes the same amount of time as a long coffee break."

At my age, I don't need to wear make-up. WWJD?

"Well, bully for you, ma'am, if you want to go to the grave looking like Dracula's grandma. But if you want to look young, then start applying make-up."

This little trip to the chip shop won't hurt, will it? WWJD?

"If you eat junk, you look like junk. People say, 'It's not my fault, it's my glands.' It's not; it's greed!"

So there you have it. That's what Joan would do!

THEY USED TO CALL IT GOSSIPING.
NOW IT'S CALLED SOCIAL
NETWORKING.

I believe in loyalty. When a woman reaches an age she likes, she should stick with it.

EVA GABOR

JUST SAY NO

WE UNDERSTAND THAT BEING A SEXY SENIOR, YOU MAY GET MORE ATTENTION THAN YOU WANT. HERE'S HOW TO TURN DOWN SOME COMMON AND CORNY CHAT-UP LINES.

I would go to the end of the earth for you.
Yes, but would you stay there?

....

Is this seat empty?
Yes, and this one will be too if you sit there.

....

May I have the last dance?
You've already had it.

....

I know how to please a woman.
Then please leave me alone.

....

Your place or mine?
Both – you go to your place, I'll go to mine.

....

Show me a
woman with both feet
firmly planted on the
ground, and I'll show
you a girl who can't
get her knickers off.

KATHY LETTE

Rhyme time

A sexy senior I knew,

Was dozing one day in her pew,

When the preacher yelled "Sin!"

She exclaimed, "Count me in,

As soon as the service is through."

MY DOCTOR SAID THAT I SHOULD KILL HALF THE PEOPLE I KNOW. WELL, NOT EXACTLY. HE TOLD ME THAT AT MY AGE I SHOULD GET RID OF THE STRESS IN MY LIFE. SAME THING REALLY...

· *SEXY TIP* ·

If someone says you are over the hill, tell them,
"Get out of my way, I'm picking up speed."

Rhyme one more time

Bigamy, they say, is a vice,

And more than one spouse is not nice,

But one is a bore,

I'd prefer three or four,

And the plural of spouse is spice!

John Bratton

Lost weekend

Friday was pension day so Rose asked her husband, Jim, to get some cash out of the bank for the week.

With the money in his wallet and the sun in the sky, Jim realized that conditions were ideal for a game of golf. After a round with his friends, he carried on with several drinks at the 19th hole. Then he stayed at a friend's house, and after a good night's sleep, the good times continued for the rest of the weekend.

When he finally appeared at home on Sunday night, Jim was confronted by an angry Rose who went at him full throttle with a tirade befitting his actions. She ended with, "How would you like it if you didn't see me for two or three days?"

Jim replied, "That would be fine with me."

Monday went by and Jim didn't see his wife.

Tuesday and Wednesday came and went much the same.

But by Thursday, the swelling had gone down just enough so he could see Rose out the corner of his left eye.

A Sexy Senior went to her dentist to have her
dentures adjusted for the fifth time.

The dentist said "OK, one last time, but no more.
There's no reason why these shouldn't fit
your mouth easily."

"Who said anything about my mouth?" the woman
answered. "They don't fit in my glass!"

Men can be a great deal of work for very little reward.

GLENDA JACKSON

21ST-CENTURY SEXY SENIOR

How many of these 21 "then and now" comparisons do you identify with?

Find out if you're a 21st-century sexy senior!

THEN	NOW
Blue rinse streaks	Pink
Pearlized nail polish	Trip to the nail salon
Shawl	Pashmina
Scholl sandals	Jimmy Choos
Pond's Cold Cream	Crème de la Mer
Sturdy undies	Agent Provocateur
Support pants	Spanx
Twin set and pearls	M&S cashmere
Shopping trolley	Online delivery
Aquarobics	Pilates
Reading a book	Writing a blog
Polaroids	Selfies

THEN	NOW
Pot of tea	Skinny latte
Bicycle	Harley-Davidson
Strolling around the Lake District	Hiking in the Himalayas
Saga cruise	Visiting the Northern Lights
Writing a love letter	Sending a saucy text
Port and orange	Prosecco
Mary Whitehouse	Mary Portas
Army & Navy	House of Fraser
Stannah stairlift	Sports car

G-strings are comfortable? They're not.
They ride up. By the end of the night you
realize you're wearing an eyepatch.

KAREN BAYLEY

63

Nostalgia: fondly remembering something you didn't care about at the time.

• SEXY TIP •

Travel the world before you look
like your passport photo.

I'M IN THE PUBLIC EYE, SO I DON'T CARE WHO KNOWS WHAT I GET DONE. IF I SEE SOMETHING SAGGING, DRAGGING, OR BAGGING, I GET IT SUCKED, TUCKED, OR PLUCKED.

DOLLY PARTON

DRIVE ON

"How was your blind date?"

"Terrible! He showed up in a 1932 Rolls-Royce."

"What's so terrible about that?"

"He was the original owner."

A little pick-me-up

A sexy senior lady knows that first impressions count. Here are some cheeky opening lines to get his heart racing.

At the gallery – You're so handsome you could make an impression on Monet.

Playing bowls – That's a strong grip, I wonder what you could do with two hands?

At the golf club – My bedroom is the only fair way to go this evening.

At the library – I think you might have mistaken me for a library book – I saw you checking me out.

At the gym – You've got me more out of breath than usual.

Archery – You've got me all a-quiver.

Gardening – You look like someone who knows his way around a clematis.

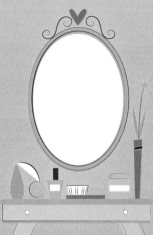

USE A MAKE-UP TABLE WITH EVERYTHING CLOSE AT HAND AND DON'T RUSH; OTHERWISE YOU'LL LOOK LIKE A PATCHWORK QUILT.

LUCILLE BALL

· SEXY TIP ·

Retirement means you can do what you want 7 nights a week.

> I'm kind of comfortable with getting older because it's better than the other option, which is being dead. So I'll take getting older.
>
> **GEORGE CLOONEY**

TOP 10 SILVER FOXES

Form an orderly queue, ladies!

George Clooney

Richard Gere

Harrison Ford

Robert Redford

Pierce Brosnan

Barack Obama

Jose Mourinho

Kevin Costner

Antonio Banderas

Hugh Laurie

TOP 10 SFTS
(SILVER FOXES IN TRAINING)

The next generation of silver foxes.
Keep an eye on these young studs...

Brad Pitt

David Beckham

Matt le Blanc

Idris Elba

Matt Damon

Ben Affleck

Ryan Gosling

Jon Hamm

Bradley Cooper

Robert Downey Jr.

I phoned my grandparents and my
grandfather said, "We saw your movie."
"Which one?" I said. He shouted, "Betty,
what was the name of that movie I didn't like?"

BRAD PITT

I DO LOVE SHOES THAT MAKE MY LEGS LONGER. I HAVE THE UPPER BODY OF SOMEONE WHO'S 5FT 8IN, SO HIGH HEELS HELP ME EVEN OUT THE DISCREPANCY.

AMY ADAMS

· SEXY TIP ·

If they say you're in your sunset years, say,
"Bring it on, my sunglasses are bifocal."

I'M TIRED OF ALL THIS NONSENSE ABOUT BEAUTY BEING ONLY SKIN-DEEP. THAT'S DEEP ENOUGH. WHAT DO YOU WANT – AN ADORABLE PANCREAS?

JEAN KERR

Sexy movies

Turn off that soap opera and stop that box set! Take a trip back to the 80s and 90s when sexy scenes set the box office alight! Which of these steamy films do you remember sneaking off to see in your younger days?

Fatal Attraction

Basic Instinct

9½ Weeks

Risky Business

The Blue Lagoon

WHY MEN LOVE DATING SEXY SENIORS

A sexy senior can wear any hat she chooses and nobody will laugh.

A young woman wearing the same hat will always look like an Ikea lampshade.

A sexy senior always carries a handbag full of emergency supplies.

A young woman will starve or quietly bleed to death at the slightest hitch.

A sexy senior will tell you that you are
an ass if you're acting like one.

A young woman will say nothing, just in case
it means you might break up with her.

A sexy senior will call you up and ask you for a date.

A young woman will wait forever,
by the phone, for you to call.

A sexy senior knows how to cook.

A young woman knows how to order
pizza on her smartphone.

A sexy senior will introduce you to all of her girlfriends.

A young woman will avoid her girlfriends when
she's with you, in case you get any ideas.

A sexy senior will never accuse you of using her.

She's using you.

Go West!

One lady who could always be relied upon for a killer one-liner was Mae West. Here's our top ten:

It's not the men in my life that count, it's the life in my men.

....

Give a man a free hand and he'll run it all over you.

....

Its hard to be funny when you have to be clean

....

I never worry about diets. The only carrots that interest me are the number you get in a diamond.

....

I used to be Snow White, but I drifted.

....

Say what you want about long dresses, but they cover a multitude of shins.

....

Ten men waiting for me at the door? Send one of them home, I'm tired.

....

I've been in more laps than a napkin.

....

I'll try anything once, twice if I like it, three times to make sure.

....

When I'm good, I'm very good. But when I'm bad I'm better.

....

LAST WILL AND TESTAMENT

*"BEING OF SOUND MIND,
I SPENT ALL MY MONEY ON
HAVING A GREAT TIME."*

I will not retire
while I've still got
my legs and my
make-up box.

BETTE DAVIS

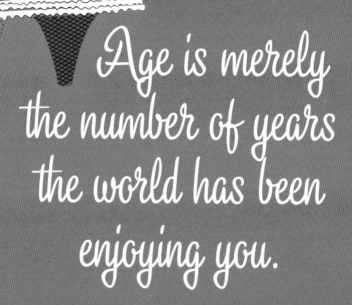

Age is merely the number of years the world has been enjoying you.

MY GRANDMOTHER WAS A VERY TOUGH WOMAN. SHE BURIED THREE HUSBANDS AND TWO OF THEM WERE JUST NAPPING.

RITA RUDNER

Under-where?

Two sexy senior ladies met up for their regular Wednesday afternoon swim. While they were changing into their swimsuits beforehand, Alice was surprised to see that Patricia was wearing gents' boxer shorts.

"I've not noticed those before," said Alice. "How long have you been wearing boxer shorts?"

Patricia replied, "Since my husband found them under the bed."

I'm not past my "youth-by" date just yet.

HISTORY VS HYT (HOT YOUNG THING)

Here are a few reasons why it is better to
date a sexy senior gentleman than an HYT:

He doesn't need
Instagram to share
sepia-toned photos.

....

The main reason a grandad
is better than an HYT?
He doesn't burn
his tongue because he
insists on drinking his tea
before everyone else
thinks it's cool.

....

He can brew his own
beer and not pay £8
a pint for "craft ale".

....

He is proud of his long-
term facial hair and not
sporting it fashionably
for a month.

....

His sailor tattoo is a
genuine pin-and-biro job
from his navy years and
not from an overpriced
tattoo parlour in
Shoreditch.

....

He will offer you his
pocket handkerchief
rather than screaming,
"Don't cry into that, it's
Mulberry Silk."

....

MEN ARE THOSE CREATURES WITH TWO LEGS AND EIGHT HANDS.

JAYNE MANSFIELD

GETTING LIPPY

Lipstick colour names are getting madder every year. Are any of these genuine colours in your sexy senior make-up bag?

Constant Toast

Stand-up Broad

Praline Blop

Whipped Caviar

Wolvesmouth

Blankety

Chunky Dunk

Celebutard

Bye bye

Every day is precious. There's no point in a sexy senior lady like you holding on to a man after his sell-by date. Here are a few choice ways to say goodbye.

I don't want you spending all your money on Viagra.

....

I know it took me 35 years to finally get you out on a date, but now I'm feeling tied down.

....

Am I having a hot flush or is this relationship suffocating me?

....

My cats don't like you.

....

I don't have time for investments with no return.

....

You're too old for me. Sorry, I mean, too young. We're the same age? Well, that doesn't work for me, either.

I've reached that age where my brain went from "You probably shouldn't say that" to "What the hell, let's see what happens".

· SEXY TIP ·

You're never too old to learn something stupid.

Out and about

You are a confident woman and proud of your years.
But you may not always want to advertise them,
especially when out and about with your chap.
Here are a few tips:

Don't read the menu and say,
"Well that won't agree with me."

....

Avoid mentioning either "Round the Horne",
your first Hillman Minx or Vera Lynn.

....

Don't mention how young your doctor is.

....

Don't sing along to the music in the lift.

....

On no account say you remember
anywhere when it was a field.

....

If you bend down to tie your shoes, don't look around
for anything else to do while you're down there.

• SEXY TIP •

You can't turn the clock back,
but you can wind it up again.

The average man is more
interested in a woman
who is interested in him
than he is in a woman
with beautiful legs.

MARLENE DIETRICH

83

MEN TALK – PART II

A few more quotes from the male perspective
on things senior and/or sexy.

Nobody will ever win the battle of the sexes.
There is too much fraternizing with the enemy.

HENRY KISSINGER

Do infants have as much fun in infancy
as adults do in adultery?

GROUCHO MARX

So, have you heard about the oyster who
went to a disco and pulled a mussel?

BILLY CONNOLLY

Older women are like aging strudels
– the crust may not be so lovely, but the
filling has come at last into its own.

ROBERT FARRAR CAPON

A man is not old until regrets take the place of dreams.

JOHN BARRYMORE

I am always looking for meaningful one-night stands.

DUDLEY MOORE

Thirty-five is a very attractive age. London society is full of women of the very highest birth who have, of their own free choice, remained thirty-five for years.

OSCAR WILDE,
THE IMPORTANCE OF BEING EARNEST

WOMEN DON'T MAKE FOOLS OF MEN; MOST OF THEM ARE THE DO-IT-YOURSELF TYPES.

Give a girl the right shoes, and she can conquer the world.

MARILYN MONROE

REMEMBER: LIFE IS AN ENDLESS STRUGGLE FULL OF FRUSTRATIONS AND CHALLENGES, BUT EVENTUALLY YOU FIND A HAIRSTYLIST YOU LIKE.

• SEXY TIP •

Don't think of it as getting hot flushes. Think of it as your inner child playing with matches.

In-action

Harold and Stan were enjoying a pint at the local British Legion Club, reminiscing about their time in the services.

"Harold," said Stan, "remember that stuff they used to give us during the war to stop us feeling randy all the time?"

"Oh, yes," chuckled Harold, "yes I do."

"Well," said Stan, "I think it's finally kicking in."

TV TAKEOVER 1

Call them glamorous grannies at your peril! These British beauties have taken over our TVs in their prime.

SHARON OSBORNE

You name it, Sharon's done it: rock band manager, TV talk show host and talent show judge. This feisty broad has a mean line in one-liners and doesn't mind throwing a glass of water or two over her male co-presenters. Now 64, Sharon's worth a whopping $220 million!

MARY BERRY

Despite being a firm favourite of the cooking masses since the 1970s, 80-something jeans-wearing super-cook, author and CBE recipient Mary Berry (and her funky floral bomber jackets) took over our TVs on The Great British Bake Off, winning a BAFTA along the way!

DAME JOAN COLLINS

Although she was a child star, wonder woman Joan Collins became a true household name as she entered her 50s playing Alexis Carrington Colby in 80s supersoap, Dynasty. Now in her 80s, she continues to tour in her one-woman stage shows, act and write books.

TV TAKEOVER 2

Superstar seniors from the US of A!

Because nothing says sexy like a powerful older woman with millions of dollars in the bank...

OPRAH WINFREY

62-year-old Oprah is the queen of US TV, with her own TV station and magazine. Her daily talk show ran for 25 years and she was nominated for a Best Supporting Actress Oscar. She's worth a massive $3.1 BILLION and her empire just keeps on growing! Go Oprah!

Quote: I still have my feet on the ground, I just wear better shoes.

KRIS JENNER

Super-hot Kris Jenner is "momager" to her six children and matriarch of the Kardashian clan. Thanks to their hit TV show, Keeping Up With the Kardashians, and other business deals, 60-year-old Kris is now worth a kool £80 million!

Quote: I like everything a certain way. I'm not somebody who can just lay back and let it happen... And I think that's what's gotten me to where I am in life.

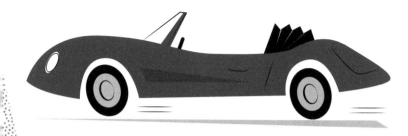

Money may
not buy happiness,
but I'd rather cry
in a Jaguar than
on a bus.

FRANÇOISE SAGAN

What are the odds!

As the hostess at the casino buffet showed me to my table, I asked her to keep an eye out for my husband, who would be joining me momentarily. I started to describe him: "He has grey hair, wears glasses, has a potbelly..."

She stopped me there. "Honey," she said, "today is senior day. They all look like that."

IN THE NEWS – BUFFING IT UP

A 69-year-old placed an ad for a "naked cleaner" in the local newsagents. They wanted someone to wash the dishes, do a bit of dusting and some general tidying – all in the buff – for £20.

They received 11 applications in the first week.

· SEXY TIP ·

It sounds quite flattering to
be called a sexagenarian.

70?
I'm 21 with
49 years'
experience!

Game over

We know just how young you are, but sometimes
it's worth playing the age card. If you are out on a
first date with a new gentleman and he's as boring
as the magazines in a dentist's waiting room,
it might be time to try one of these lines:

My nursing home closes
the front door at 8pm.

....

The parking ticket
has run out on my
mobility scooter.

....

I have to worm my 14 cats.

....

I need to revise before my
blood test tomorrow.

....

I need to get to bed, I have
a bowls match first thing
in the morning.

....

I need to put my porcelain
owl collection into
alphabetical order.

....

My bus pass expires
in 30 minutes.

....

WHY IT'S GREAT TO DATE A SENIOR MAN...

Neither his eyes nor his heart
will see your imperfections.

. . . .

You don't need to worry about meeting his parents.

. . . .

At this stage, he's not going to change.

. . . .

If he's not bald now he never will be.

. . . .

He's unlikely to stray – you're out of his league.

*IF YOU WANT A MAN
TO NOTICE YOU, JUST
WEAR RED LIPSTICK.*

MONICA BELLUCCI

94

I don't feel like I am 66 at all. I feel more like I am 35. But I have a bus pass so it must be true.

JOANNA LUMLEY

Age does not protect you from love, but love, to some extent, may protect you from age.

JEANNE MOREAU